HAL LEONARD
GUITAR METHOD
Supplement to Any Guitar Method

LE

T0048277

BY GREG KOCH

	PAGE

PLAYBACK+
Speed • Pitch • Balance • Loop

To access audio visit:
www.halleonard.com/mylibrary
Enter Code
5293-3551-8491-3544

The accompanying audio was recorded by Greg Koch using a Fender Custom Shop Stratocaster guitar and Fender Cyber Deluxe amp.
For more information on Greg Koch go to www.gregkoch.com

ISBN 978-0-634-04847-0

HAL•LEONARD®
CORPORATION
7777 W. BLUEMOUND RD. P.O. BOX 13819 MILWAUKEE, WI 53213

In Australia Contact:
Hal Leonard Australia Pty. Ltd.
22 Taunton Drive P.O. Box 5130
Cheltenham East, 3192 Victoria, Australia
Email: ausadmin@halleonard.com

Visit Hal Leonard Online at
www.halleonard.com

INTRODUCTION

Are you tired of playing the same old licks over and over again when you take a solo on guitar? *Lead Licks* is a unique book designed to increase your improvising vocabulary by taking a short phrase, or *lick*, and "morphing" it into different styles. A lick may begin in one genre, but with note choice modification, slides vs. bends, and other stylistic nuances, the idea transforms into rock, blues, country, or jazz. (There's even an "outside" version of each lick—a modern improvisational tool that started in jazz but has also been employed by many "jam band" guitarists, which takes the listener on a brief voyage beyond the given tonality, or key, and then resolves, providing a "tension and release" that can be very exciting.)

Lead Licks covers major, minor, and dominant seventh licks, plus a special "exotic" licks section—so you'll have a lick for nearly any musical situation. All in all, there are 220 licks, giving you 220 extremely effective tools for improvising! Not only will this book be a great reference for building up your soloing arsenal, but its approach of stylistic morphing may well inspire you to mutate licks already in your own trick bag!

ABOUT THE LICKS

The licks in this book were inspired by a host of artists in a variety of genres. All are relatively short so they can be quickly learned and easily digested. While there is some variety from style to style, basically the licks break down as follows:

- *Major licks* are based on the major scale or the major pentatonic, with some added chromatic ideas when necessary.
- *Minor licks* are based mostly on the Dorian mode, the minor pentatonic scale, or the blues scale, with chromatic additions.
- *Dominant seventh licks* use the Mixolydian mode or the blues scale, with occasional chromatic digressions.

The whole tone and diminished scales also appear from time to time to take a lick "outside." The exotic licks utilize a range of scales, most of which are self-explanatory—with the exception of "Raga," based on an East Indian-flavored scale consisting of the root, major third, fourth, fifth, and flatted seventh, and "Koto," based on an Oriental-sounding scale consisting of root, flatted second, fourth, fifth, and flatted sixth.

HOW TO USE THIS BOOK

There is no right or wrong way to use this book. Some people may want to learn all the licks and go through the book cover to cover; others may want to pick and choose as they please. Since soloing is such a personal form of expression and tastes vary, a previewing of the licks by listening to the audio is probably the best way to begin. Listen while following along in the book to identify and prioritize which licks really catch the ear.

After identifying a lick (or group of licks) that you want to add to your arsenal, it's best to learn it slowly, so that you can digest it without errors. On the audio, each lick is played twice; first at performance tempo, and then again at a slower practice pace. If you've learned the lick on an unamplified electric guitar, be sure to practice it "plugged in" so that you're aware of the need for proper dampening. If a lick is particularly challenging, practice it with a metronome at a speed that allows you to play it perfectly. Gradually increase the tempo of the metronome as your technique allows—but don't rush it! Impatience breeds sloppiness.

In using these licks to solo, it takes a certain incubation period to utilize any new information in a way that's musical and spontaneous. You don't want to put a lick into a solo just for the sake of it. In the same way that you may learn a new $50 word, you want to use it when it's appropriate and effective; if you tried to put it in every sentence, it would get old in a hurry. The best way to try to achieve a more musical result—after thoroughly practicing a lick so that it's effortless—is to put yourself in as many "jam" situations as you can. The more you're able to actually practice improvising, preferably with other people, the more your timing, dynamics, and spontaneity can develop. Even if your only access to jamming is to record a track of yourself playing rhythm and playing over it, or playing along with a record, the more you do it, the more of an effective improvisor you will be.

Now let's have at it!

LICK 1

TRACK 1

ROCK

BLUES

JAZZ

COUNTRY

OUTSIDE

LICK 2

TRACK 2

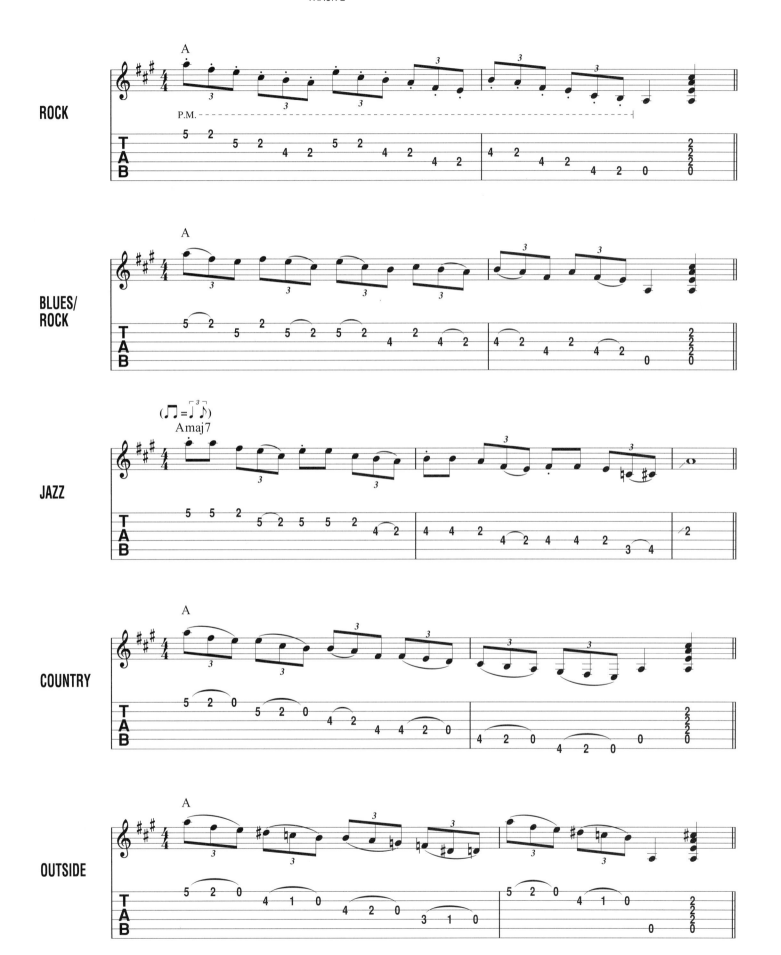

ROCK

BLUES/
ROCK

JAZZ

COUNTRY

OUTSIDE

LICK 3

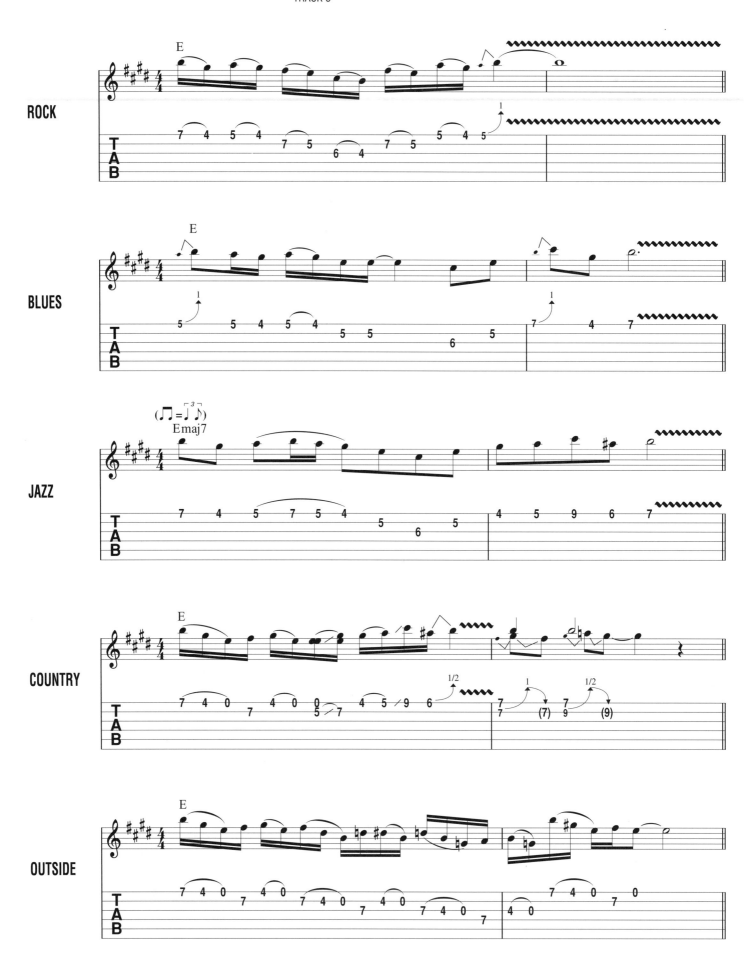

ROCK

BLUES

JAZZ

COUNTRY

OUTSIDE

LICK 4

TRACK 4

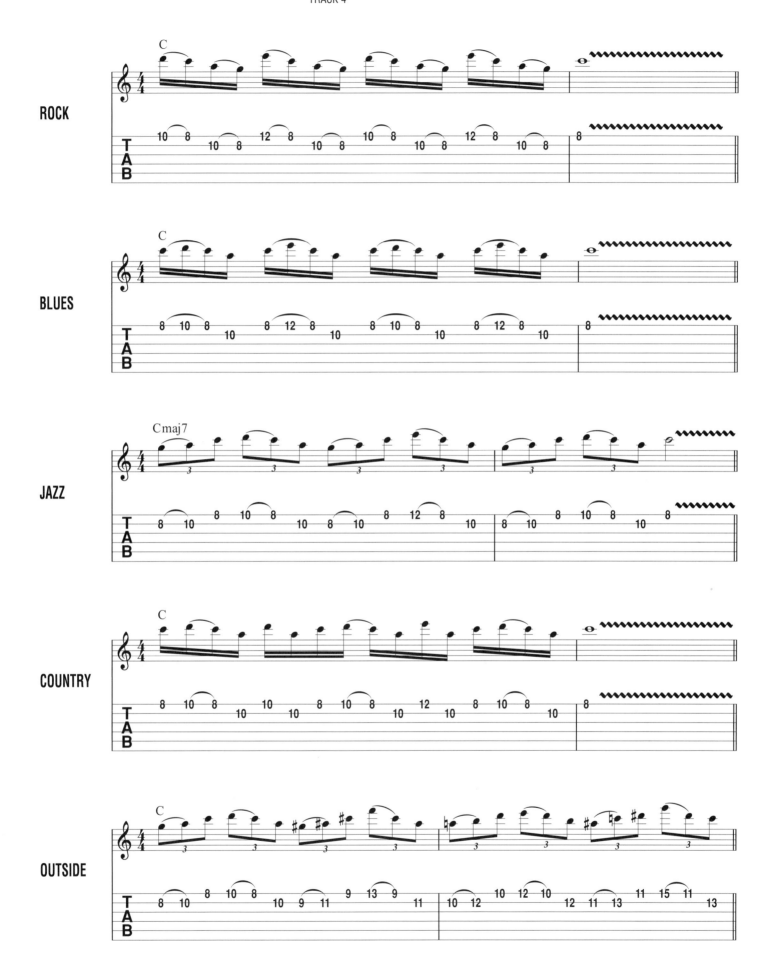

LICK 5

TRACK 5

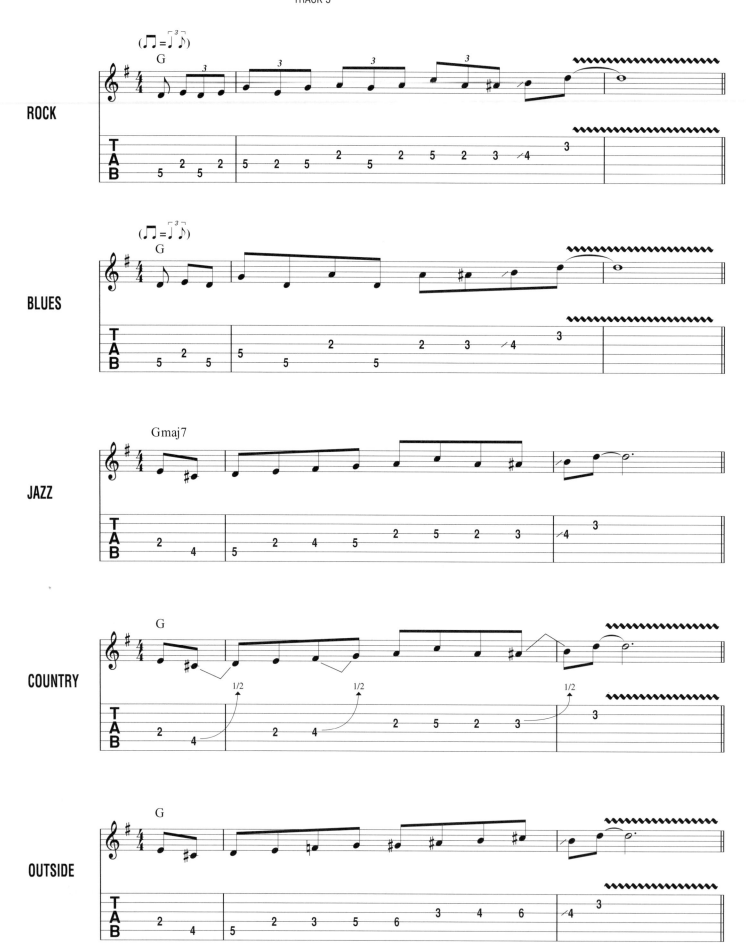

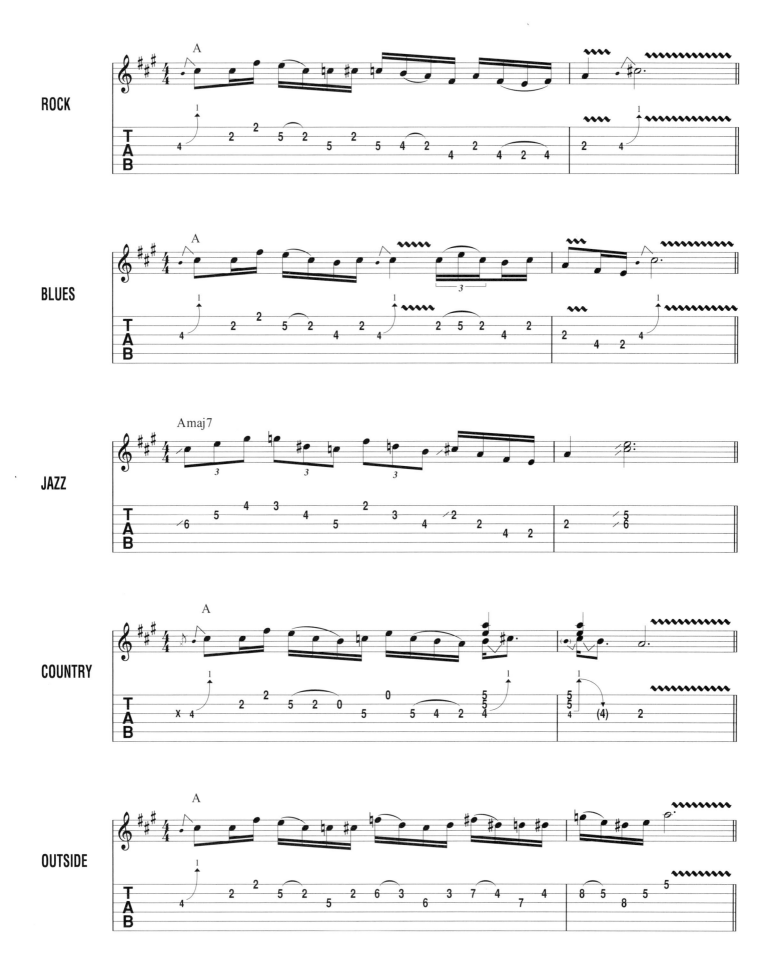

ROCK

BLUES

JAZZ

COUNTRY

OUTSIDE

LICK 7

TRACK 7

ROCK

BLUES

JAZZ

COUNTRY

OUTSIDE

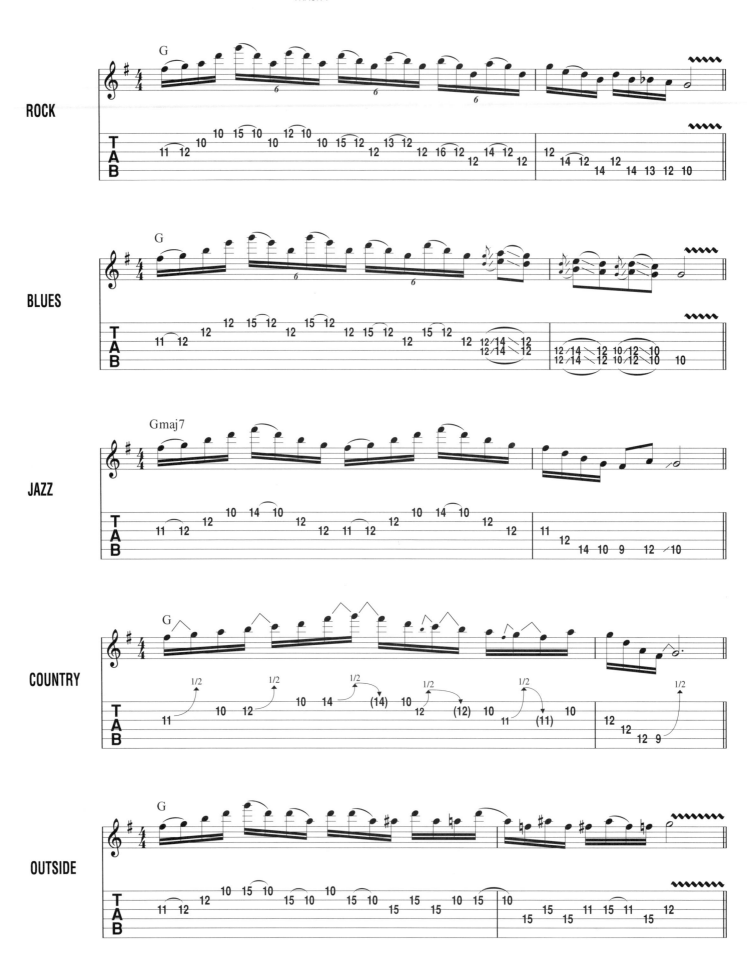

LICK 8

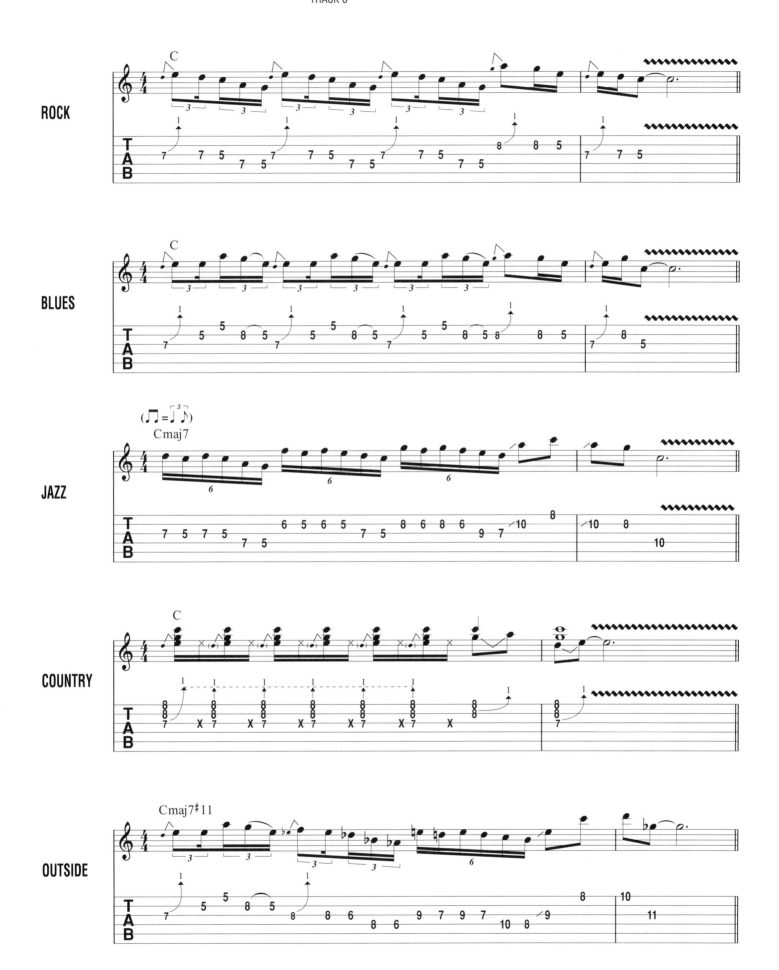

LICK 9

TRACK 9

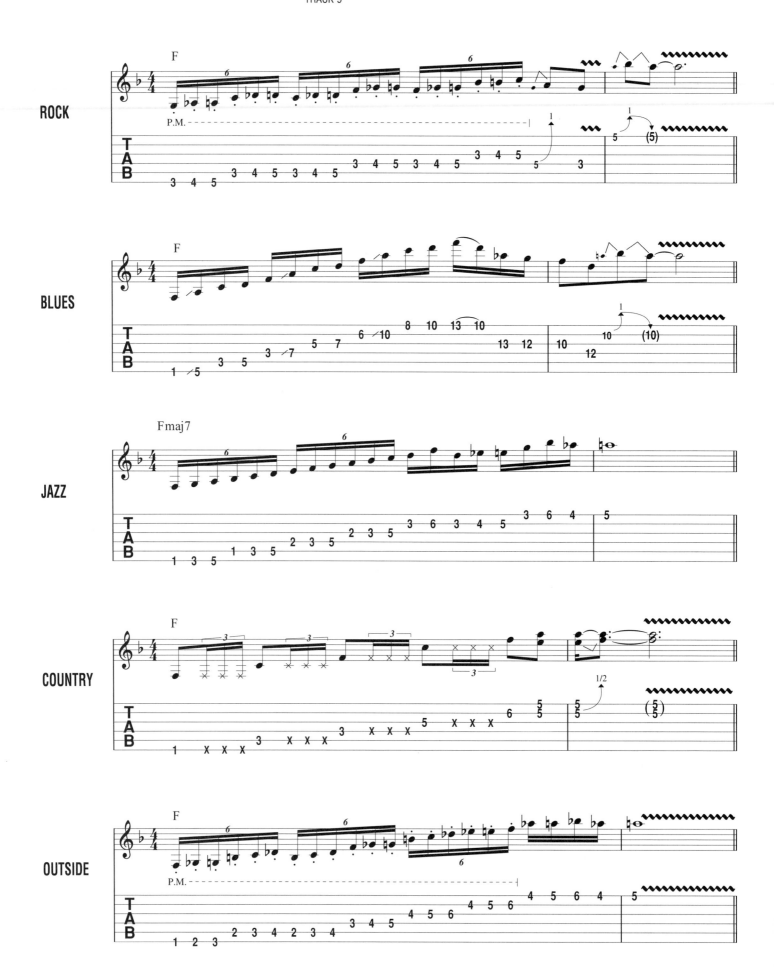

ROCK

BLUES

JAZZ

COUNTRY

OUTSIDE

LICK 10

TRACK 10

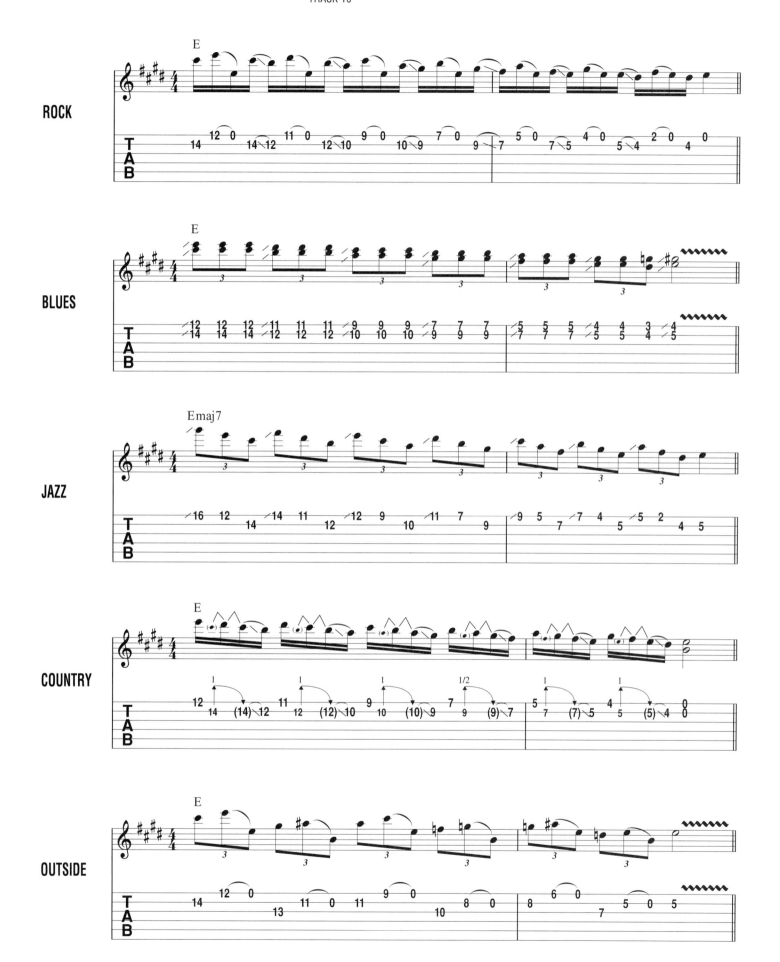

 **LICK 11**
TRACK 11

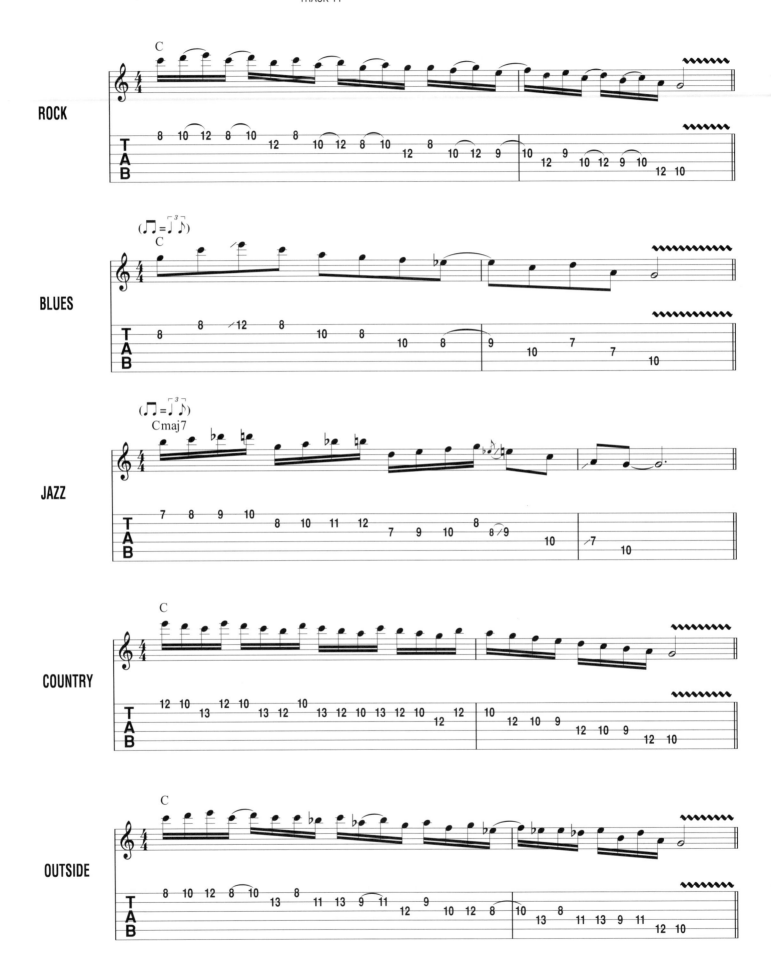

ROCK

BLUES

JAZZ

COUNTRY

OUTSIDE

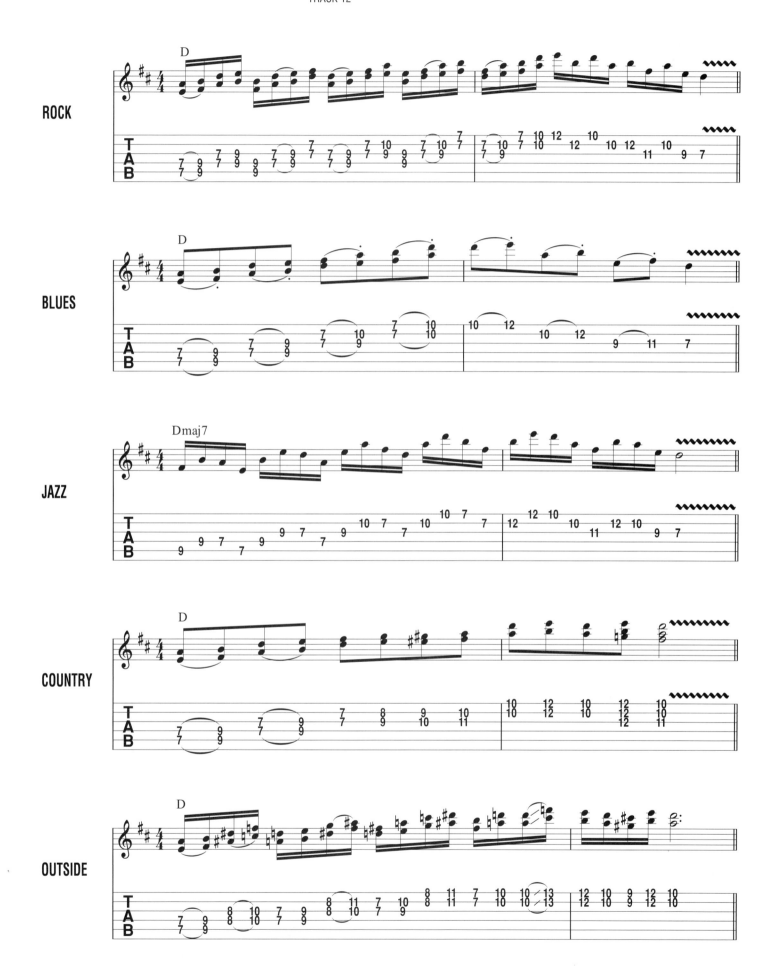

ROCK

BLUES

JAZZ

COUNTRY

OUTSIDE

 **LICK 13**

TRACK 13

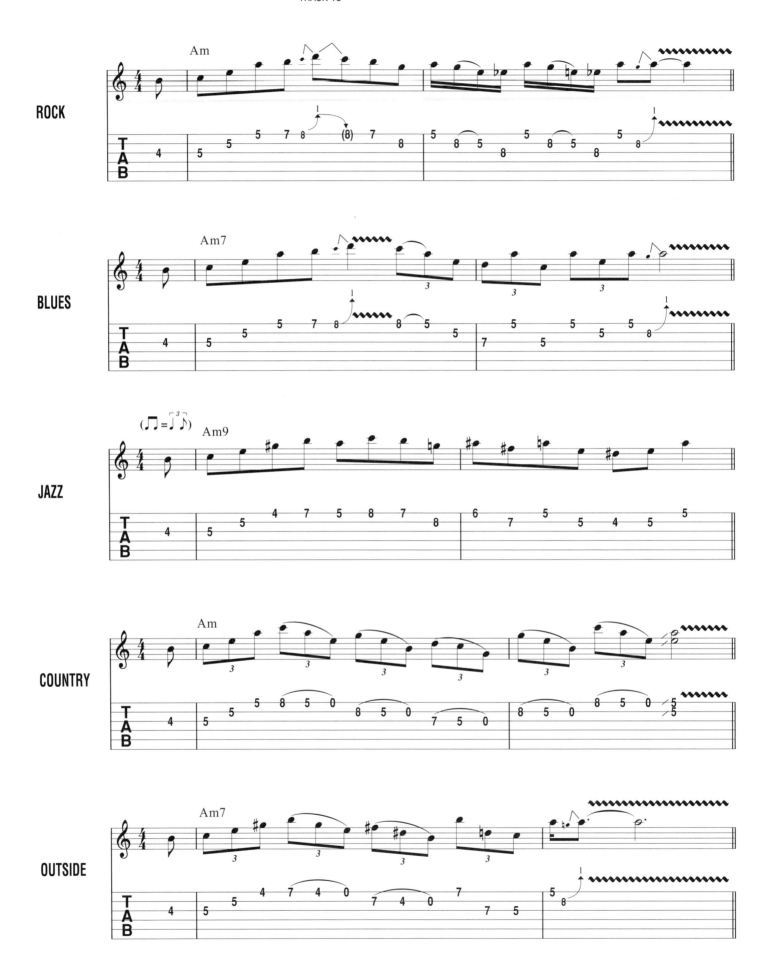

ROCK

BLUES

JAZZ

COUNTRY

OUTSIDE

LICK 14

TRACK 14

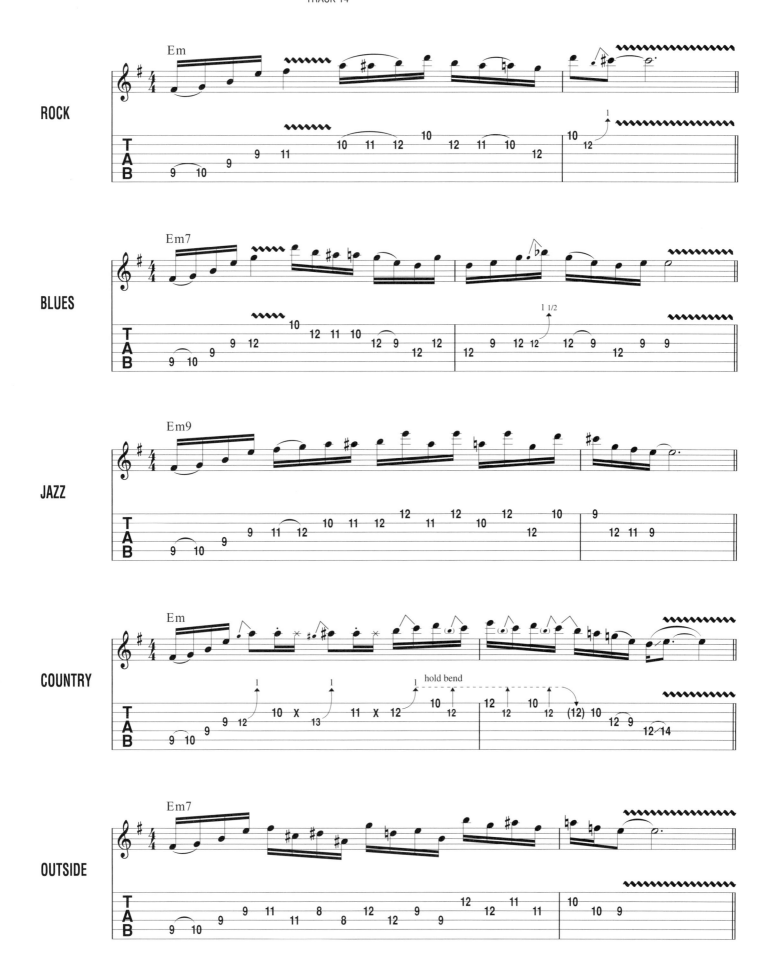

LICK 15

TRACK 15

ROCK

BLUES

JAZZ

COUNTRY

OUTSIDE

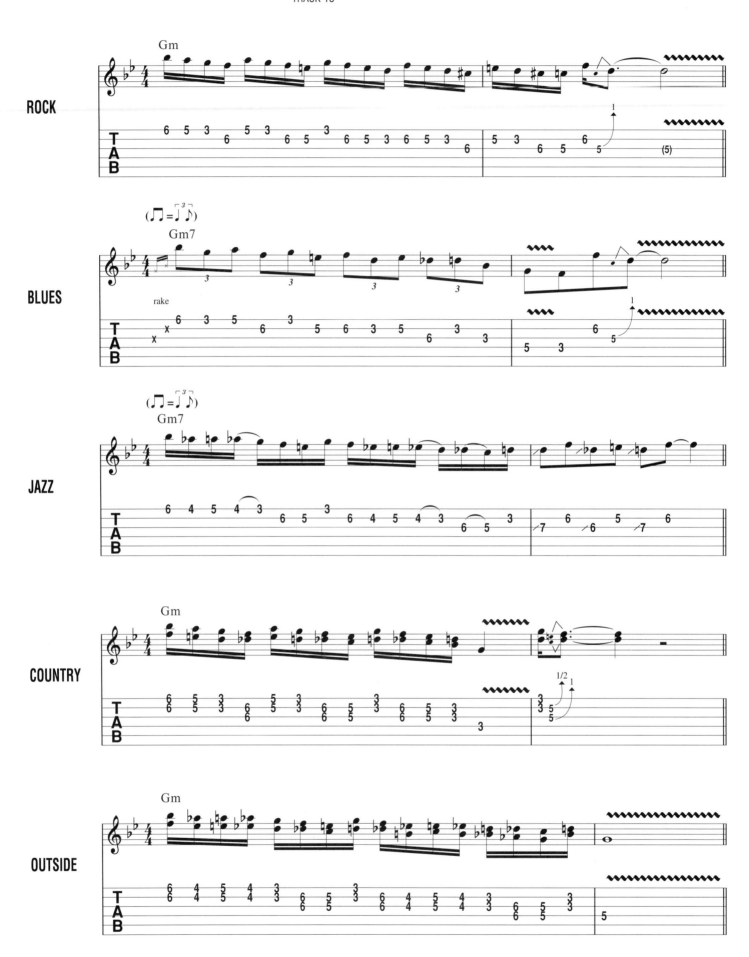

LICK 16

TRACK 16

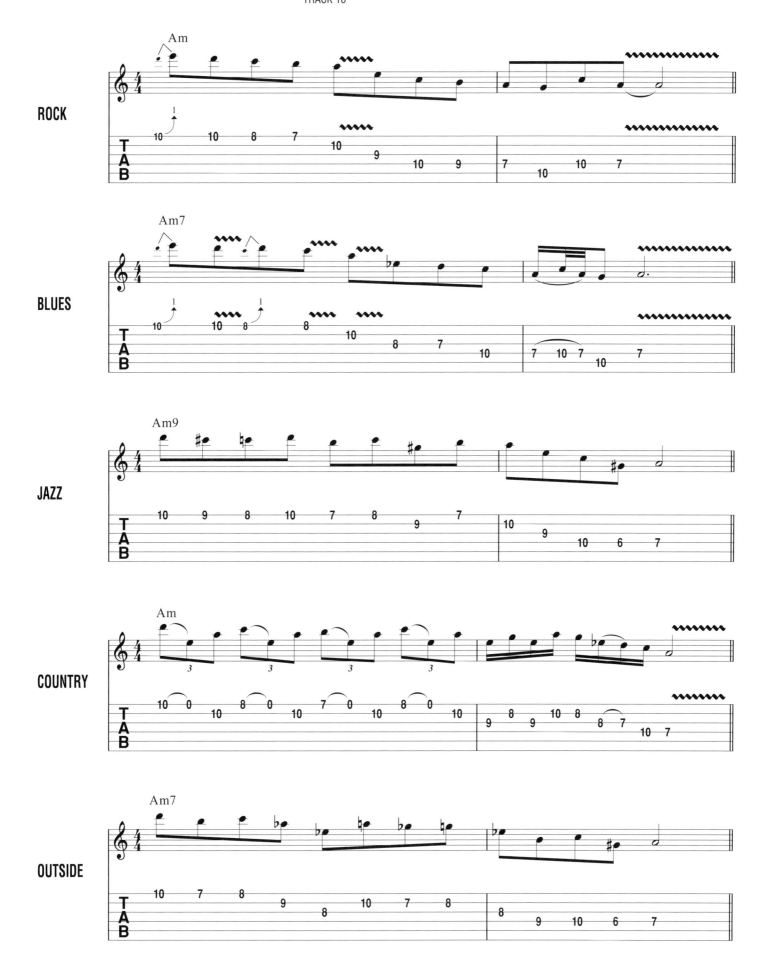

ROCK

BLUES

JAZZ

COUNTRY

OUTSIDE

LICK 17

TRACK 17

ROCK

BLUES

JAZZ

COUNTRY

OUTSIDE

 **LICK 18**
TRACK 18

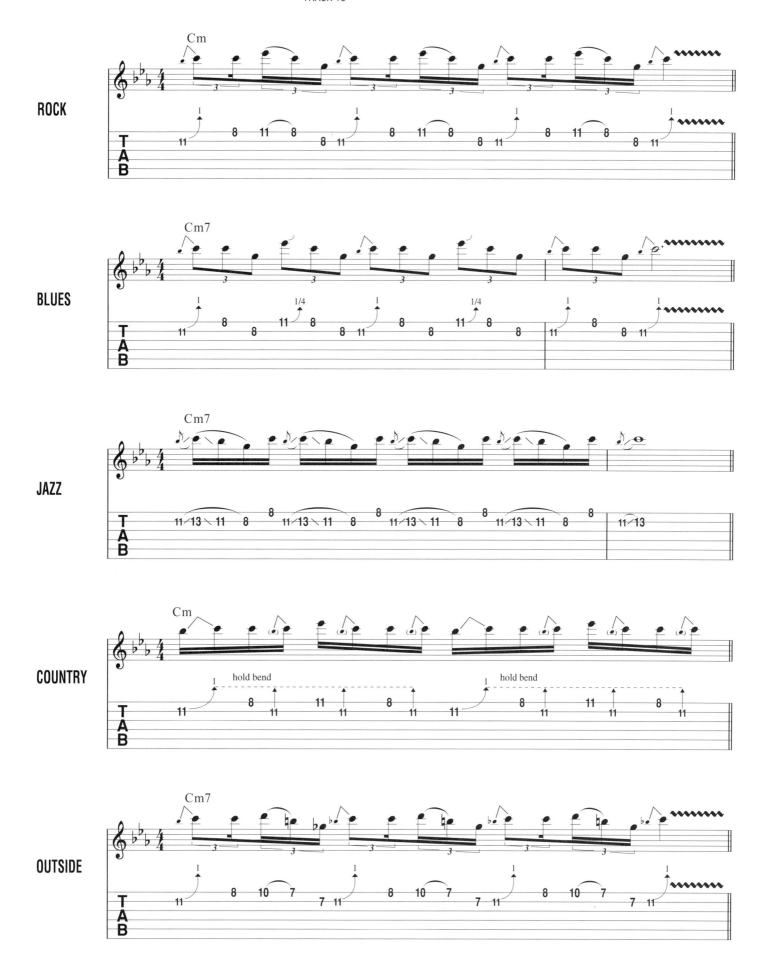

LICK 19

TRACK 19

ROCK

BLUES

JAZZ

COUNTRY

OUTSIDE

LICK 20

TRACK 20

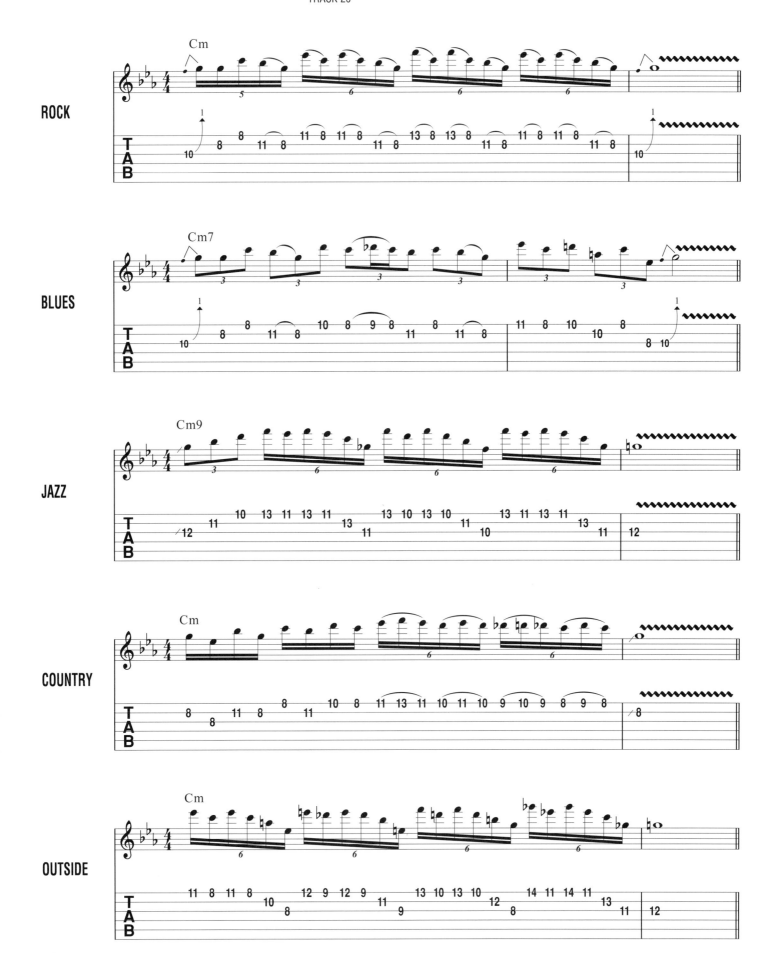

ROCK

BLUES

JAZZ

COUNTRY

OUTSIDE

LICK 21

TRACK 21

ROCK

BLUES

JAZZ

COUNTRY

OUTSIDE

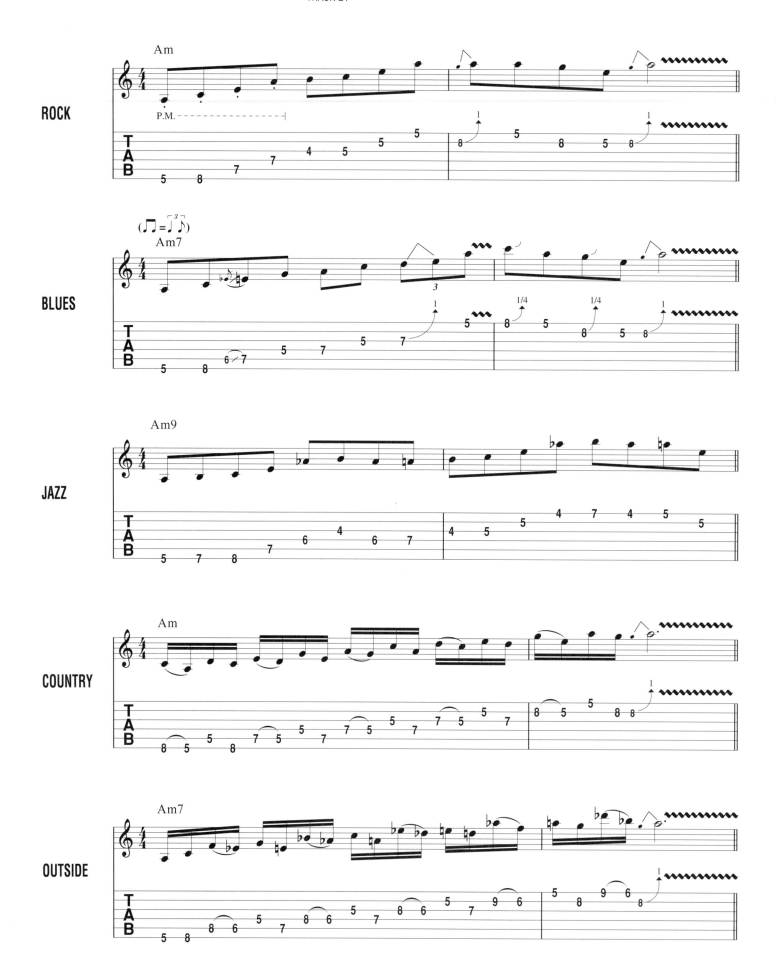

LICK 22

TRACK 22

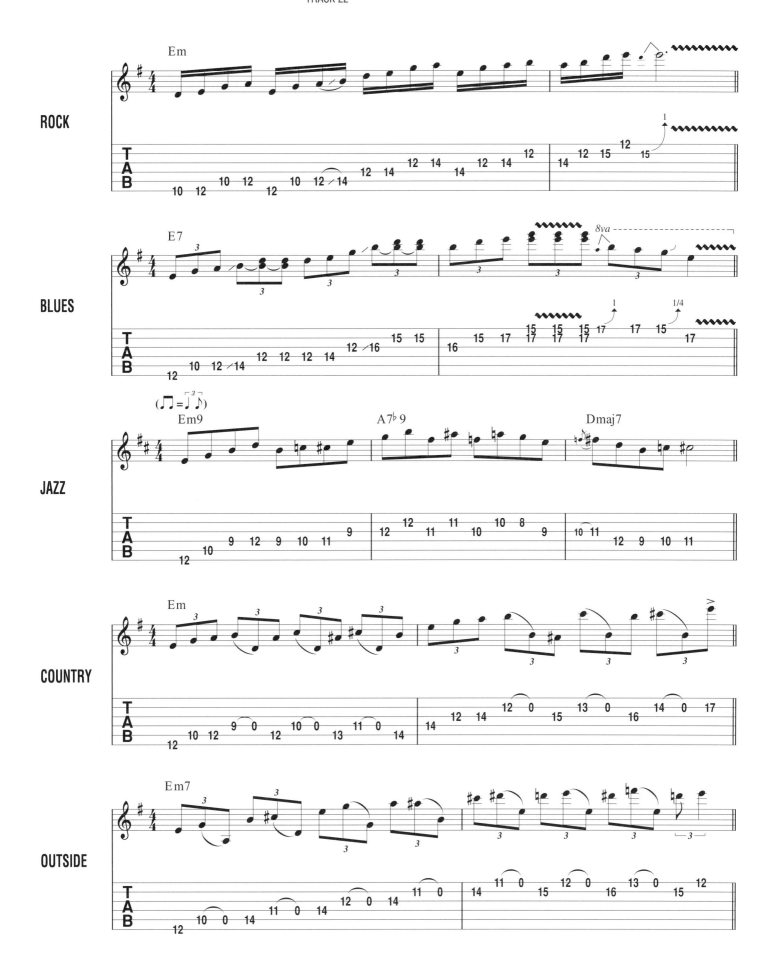

ROCK

BLUES

JAZZ

COUNTRY

OUTSIDE

LICK 23

TRACK 23

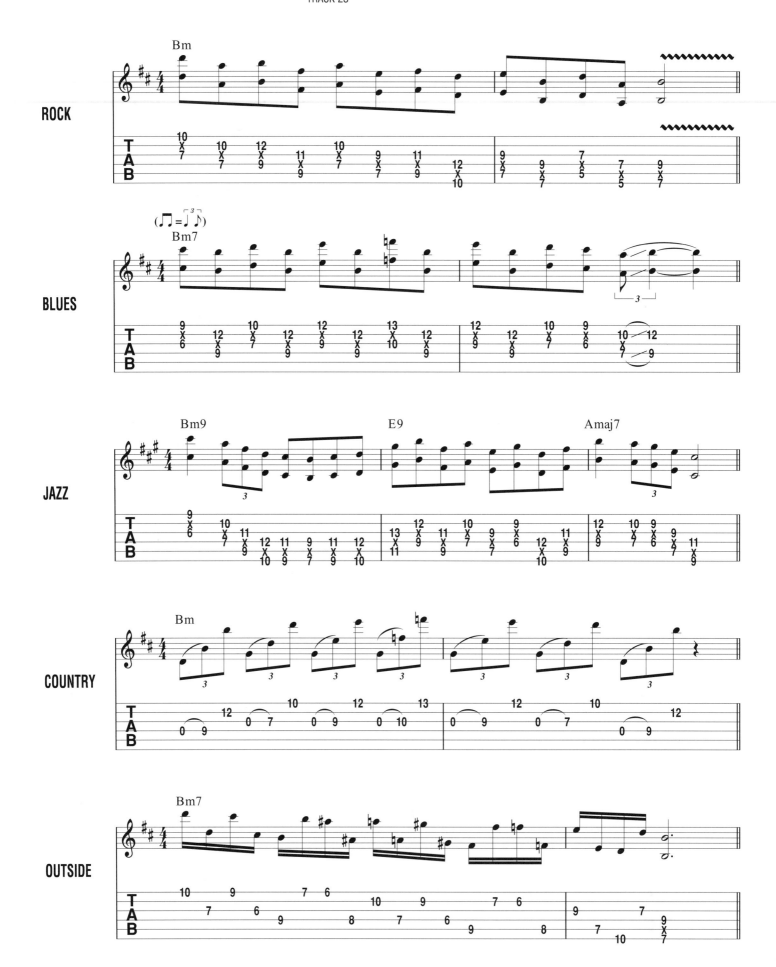

ROCK

BLUES

JAZZ

COUNTRY

OUTSIDE

LICK 24

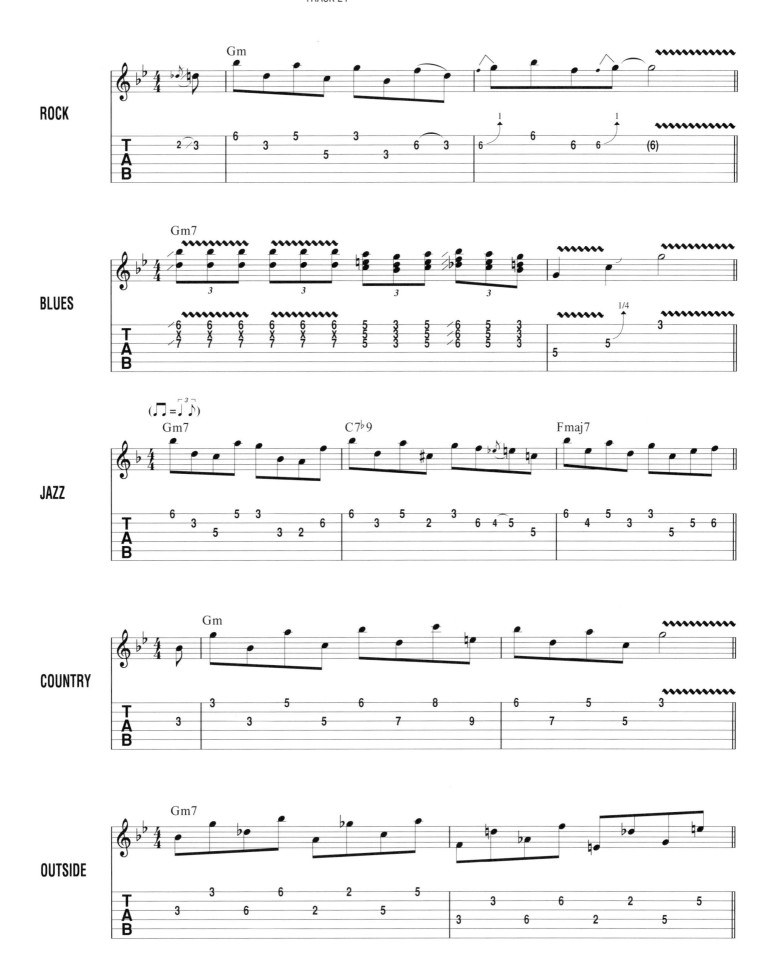

ROCK

BLUES

JAZZ

COUNTRY

OUTSIDE

LICK 25

TRACK 25

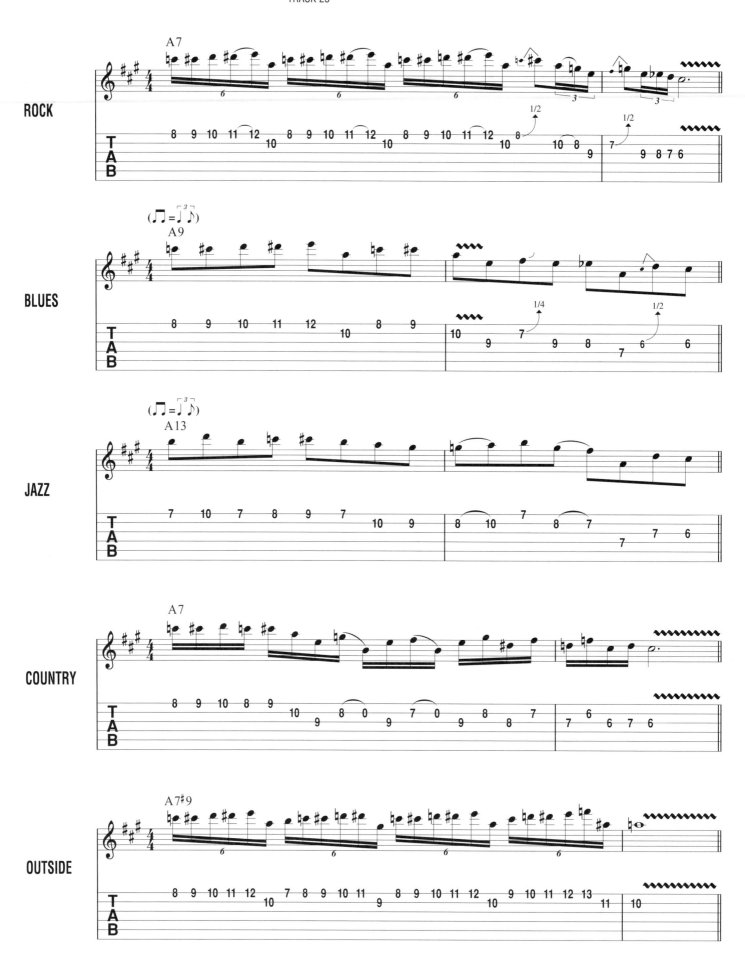

ROCK

BLUES

JAZZ

COUNTRY

OUTSIDE

 **LICK 26**

TRACK 26

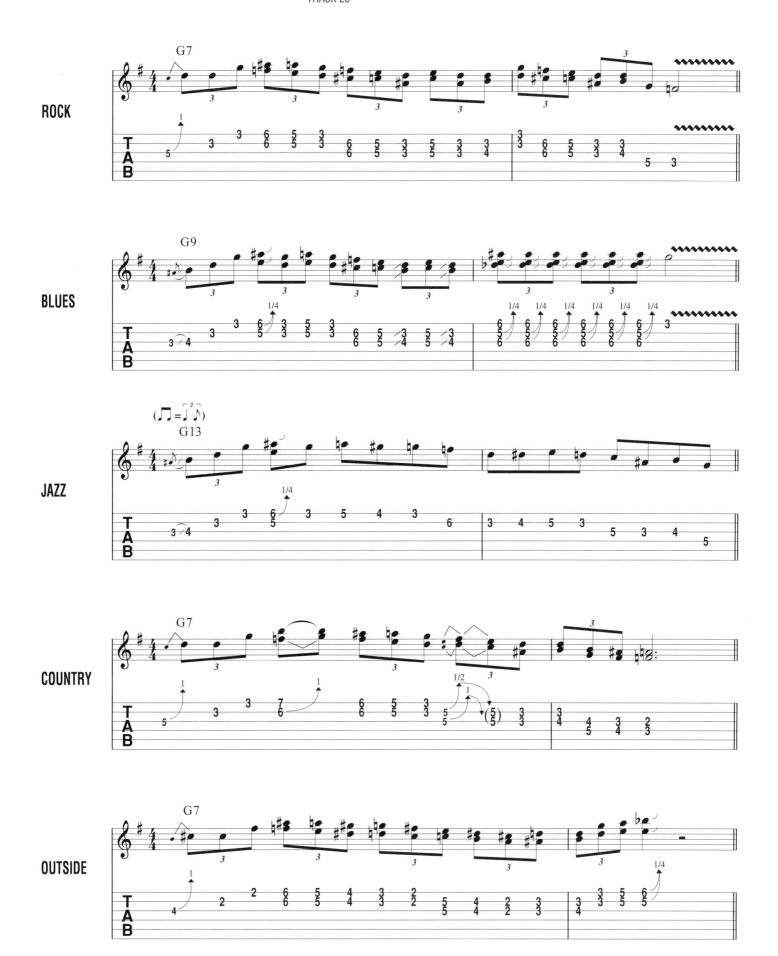

LICK 27

TRACK 27

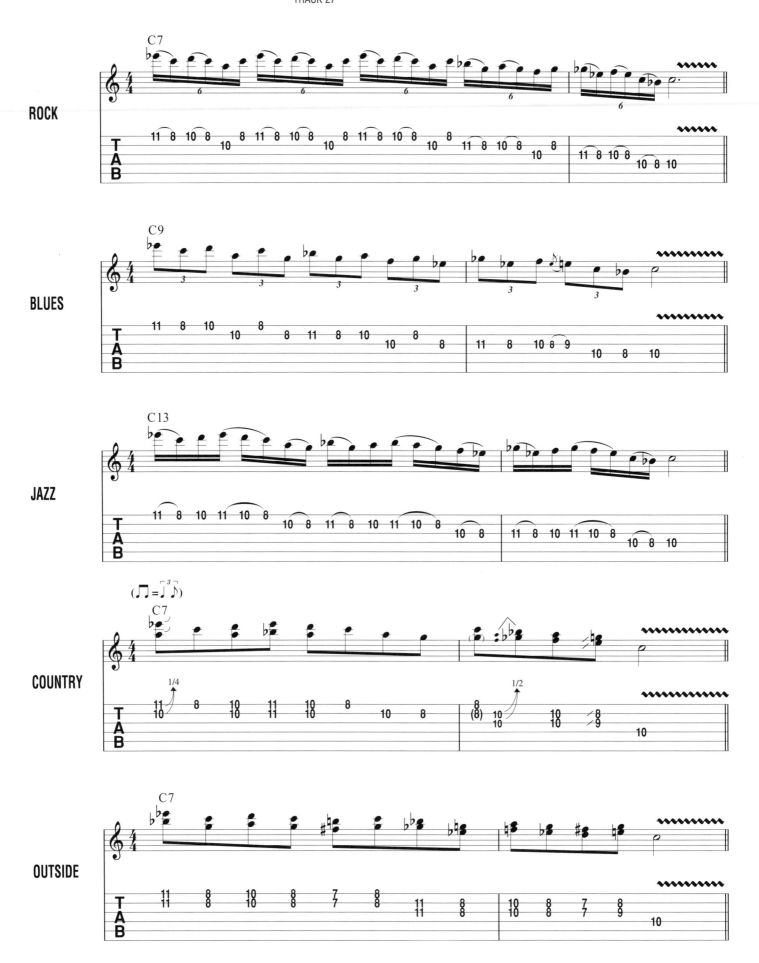

ROCK

BLUES

JAZZ

COUNTRY

OUTSIDE

LICK 28

TRACK 28

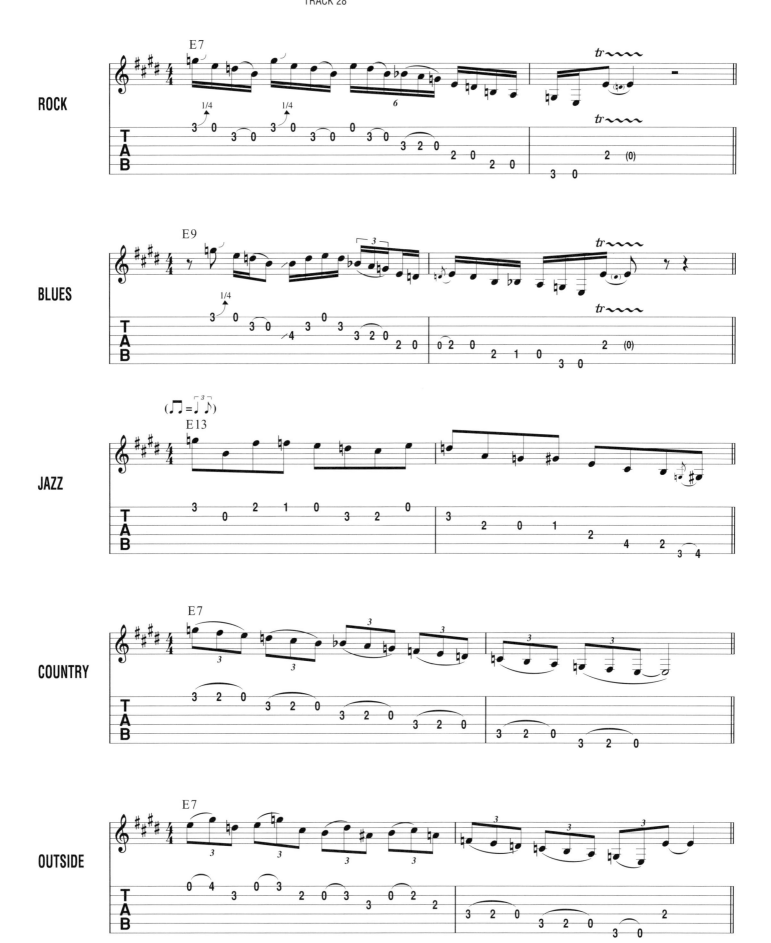

ROCK

BLUES

JAZZ

COUNTRY

OUTSIDE

LICK 29

TRACK 29

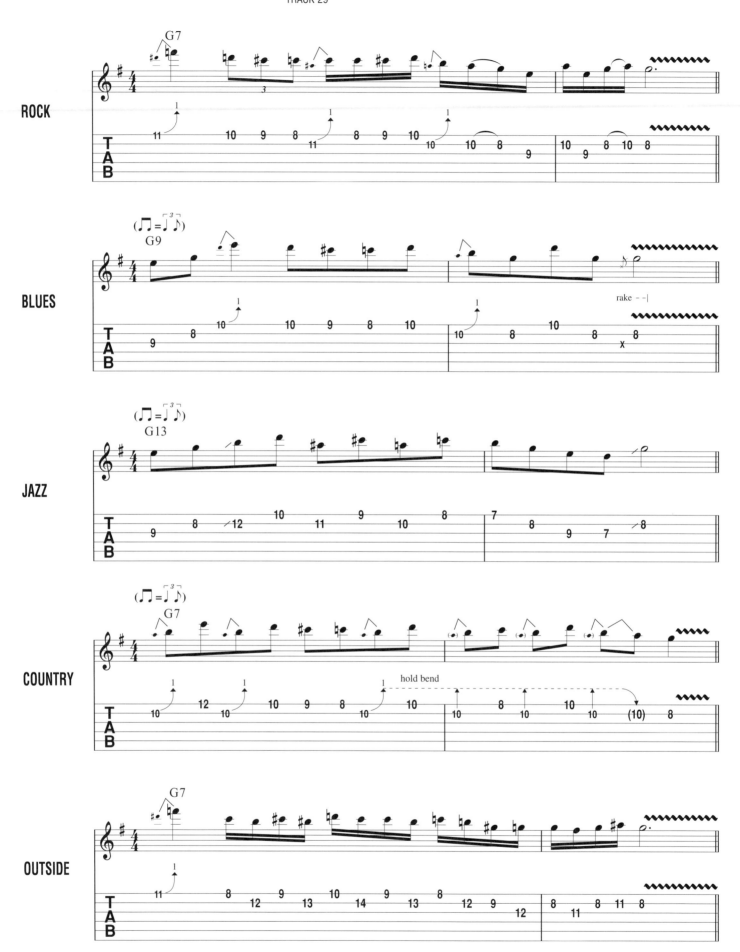

ROCK

BLUES

JAZZ

COUNTRY

OUTSIDE

LICK 30

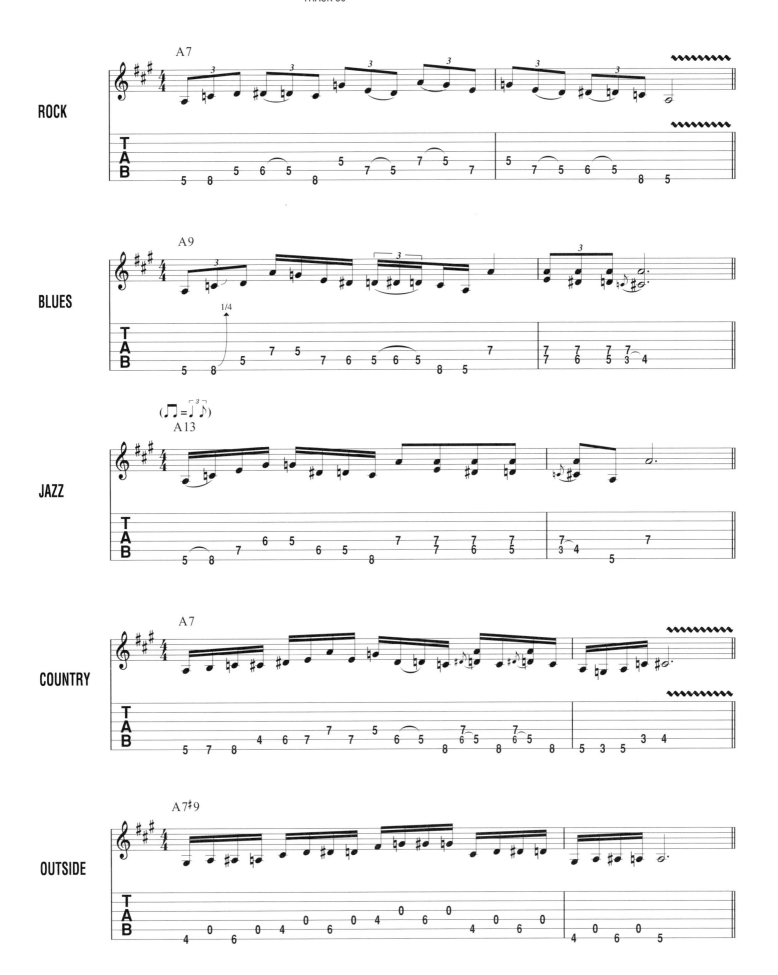

ROCK

BLUES

JAZZ

COUNTRY

OUTSIDE

🔊 LICK 31
TRACK 31

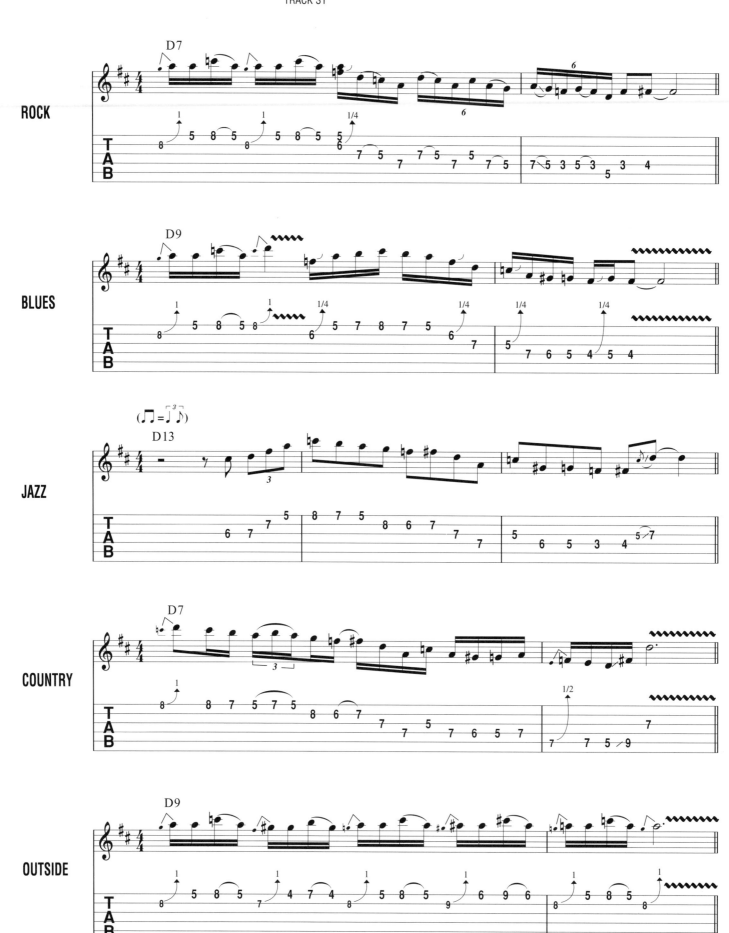

ROCK

BLUES

JAZZ

COUNTRY

OUTSIDE

 **LICK 32**
TRACK 32

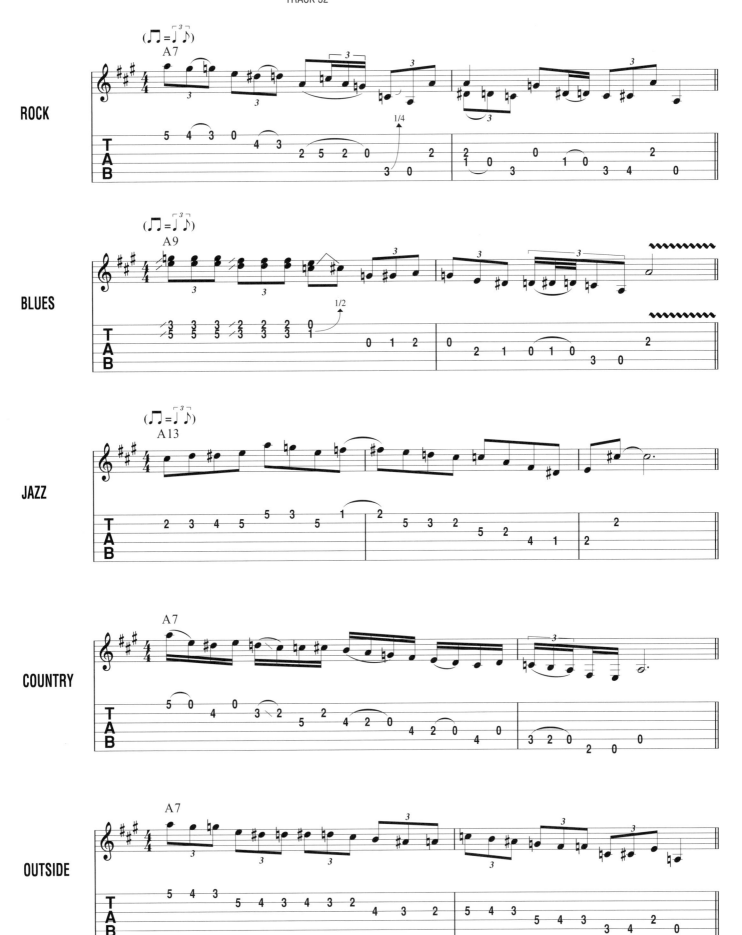

ROCK

BLUES

JAZZ

COUNTRY

OUTSIDE

 # LICK 33
TRACK 33

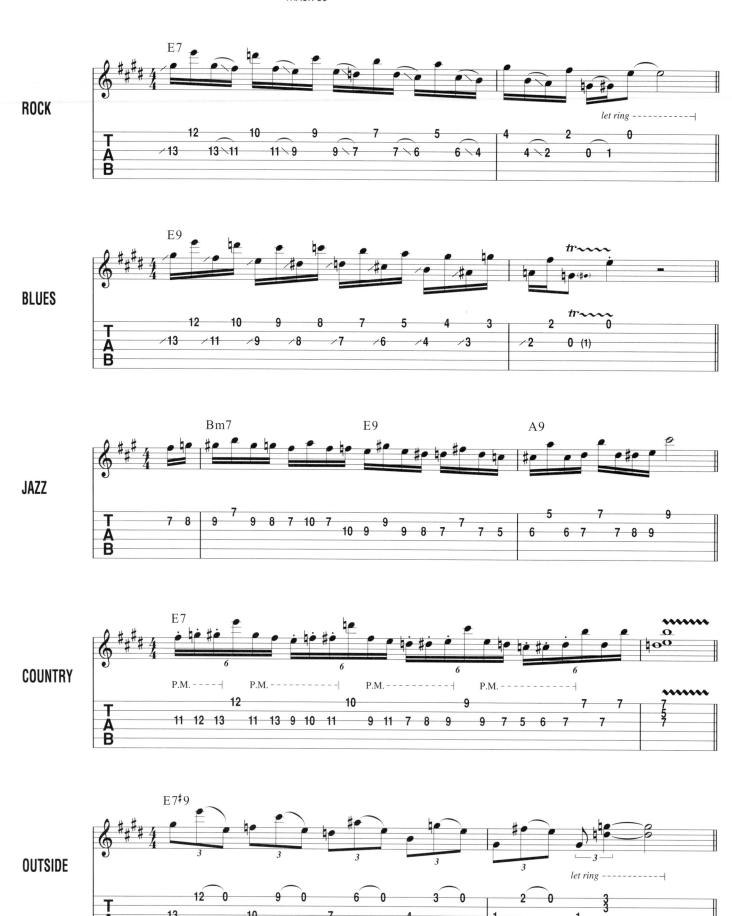

ROCK

BLUES

JAZZ

COUNTRY

OUTSIDE

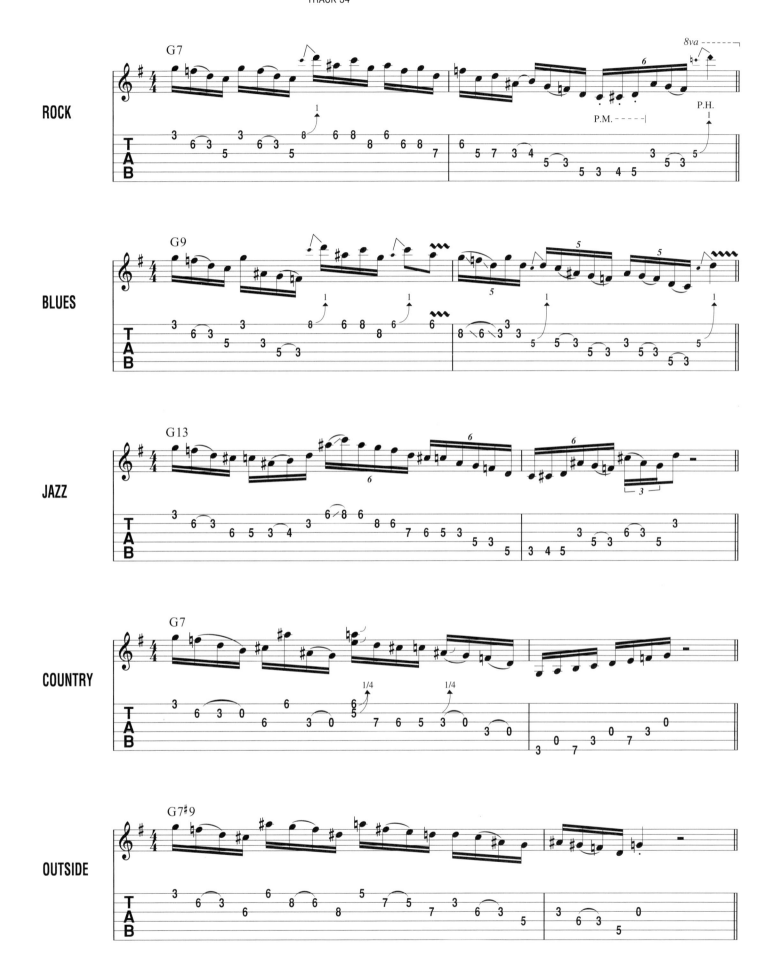

LICK 35

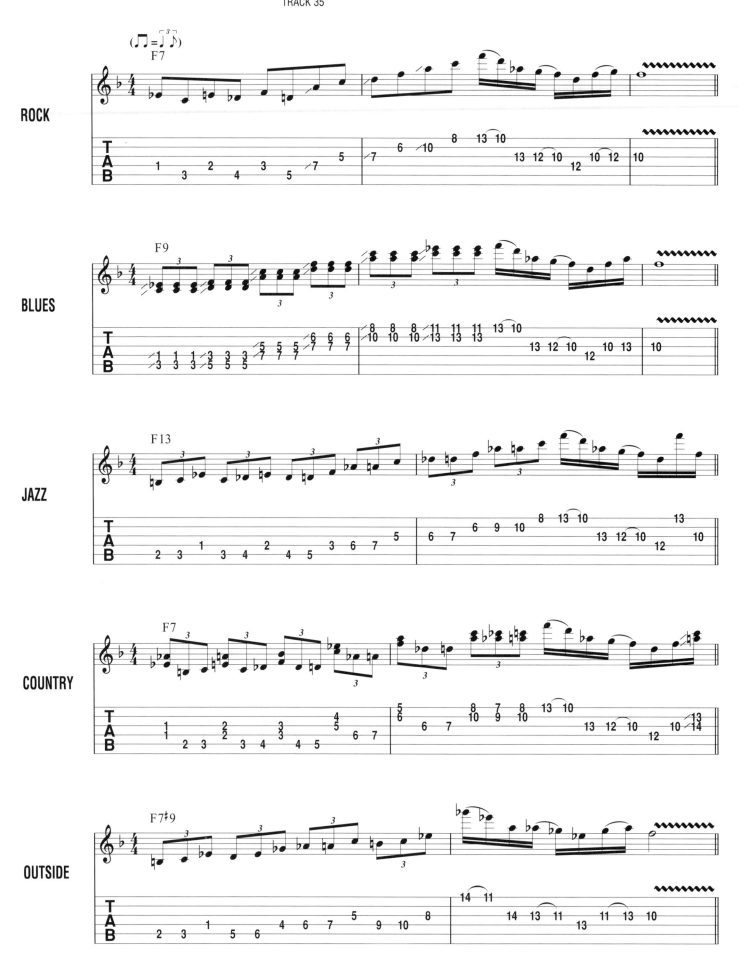

ROCK

BLUES

JAZZ

COUNTRY

OUTSIDE

LICK 36

TRACK 36

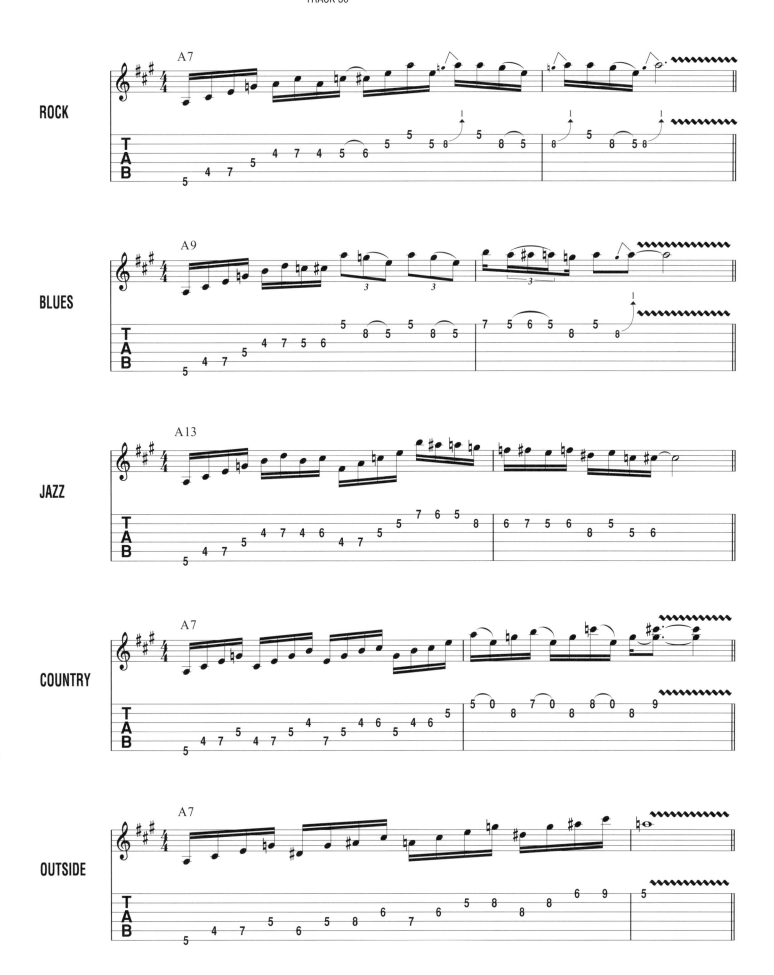

 **LICK 37**
TRACK 37

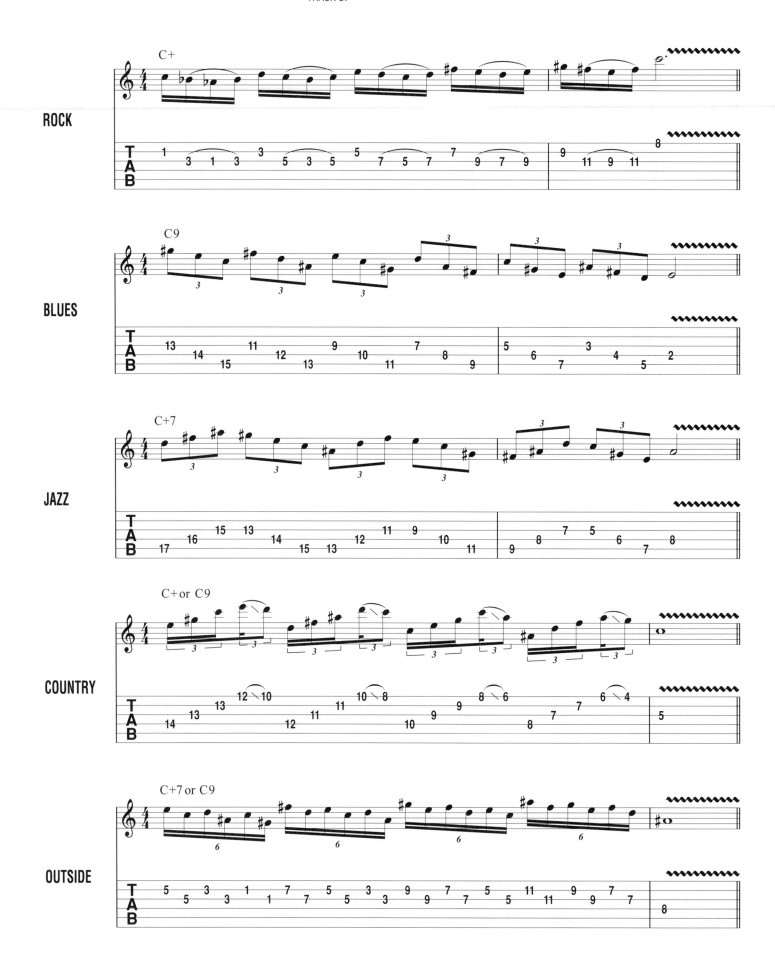

LICK 38
TRACK 38

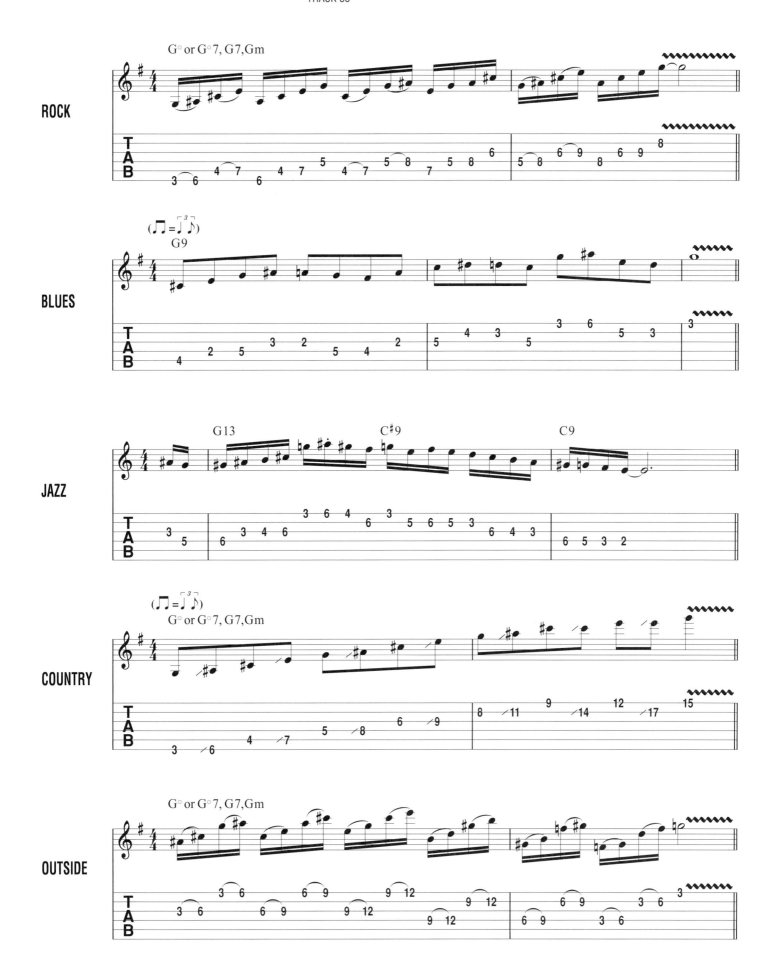

LICK 39

TRACK 39

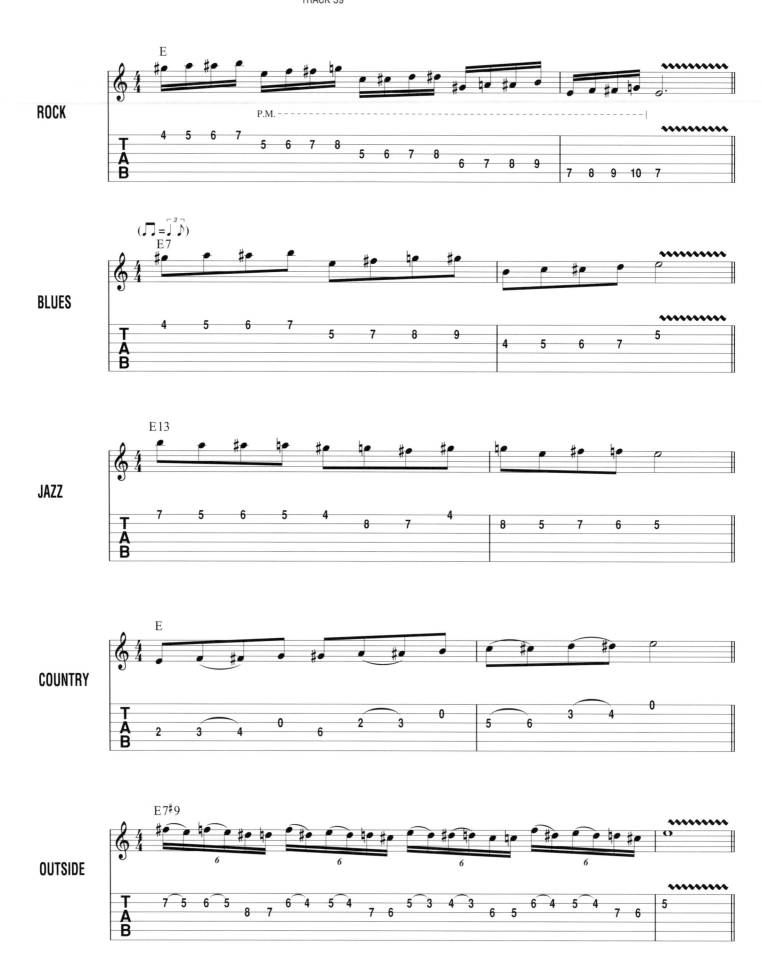

ROCK

BLUES

JAZZ

COUNTRY

OUTSIDE

LICK 40

TRACK 40

ROCK

BLUES

JAZZ

COUNTRY

OUTSIDE

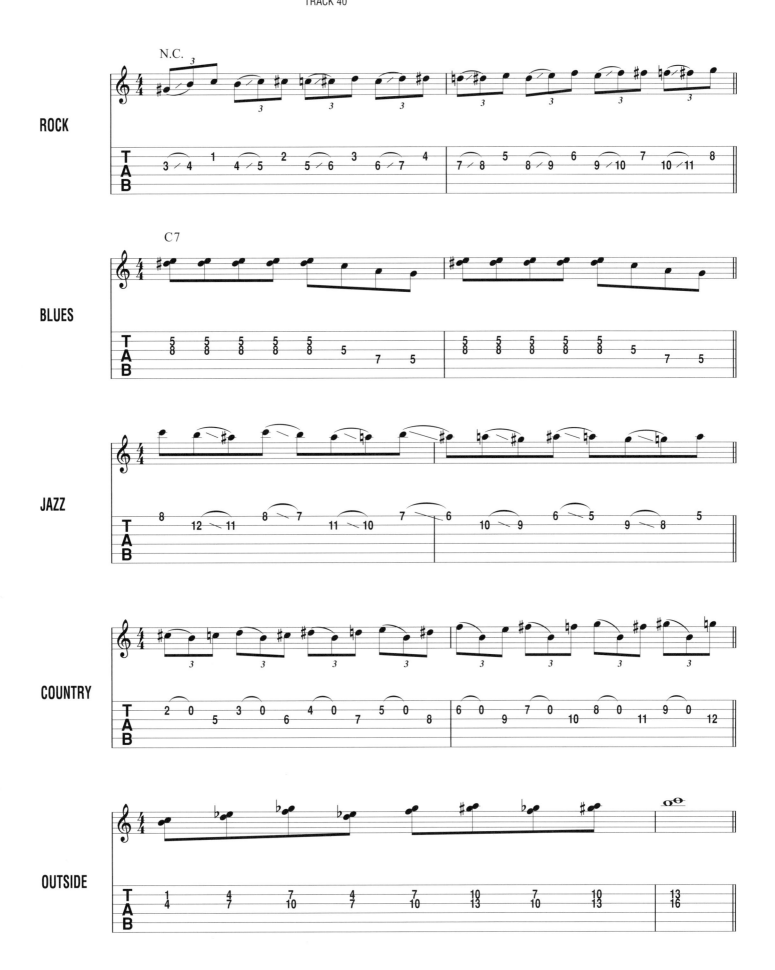

 **LICK 41**
TRACK 41

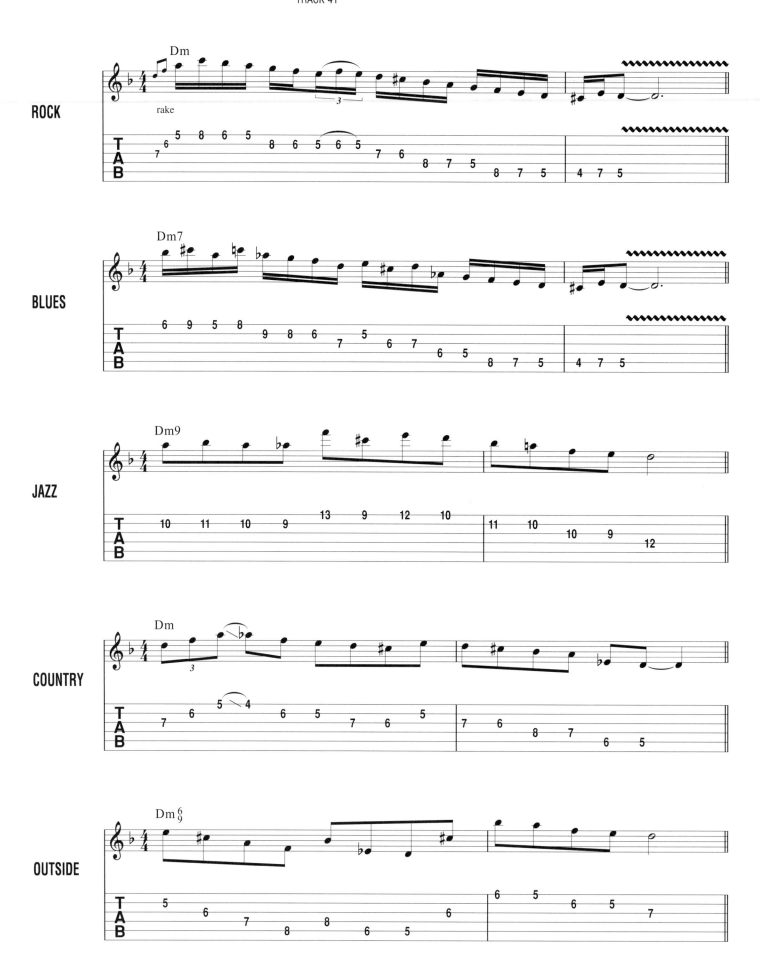

LICK 42

TRACK 42

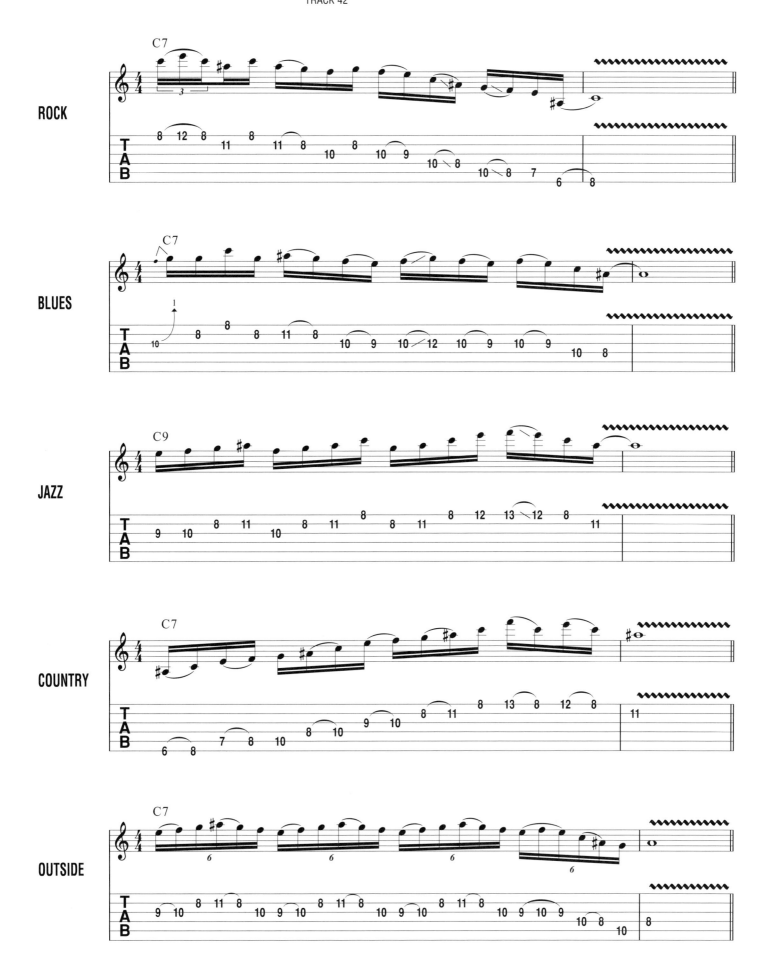

ROCK

BLUES

JAZZ

COUNTRY

OUTSIDE

LICK 43

TRACK 43

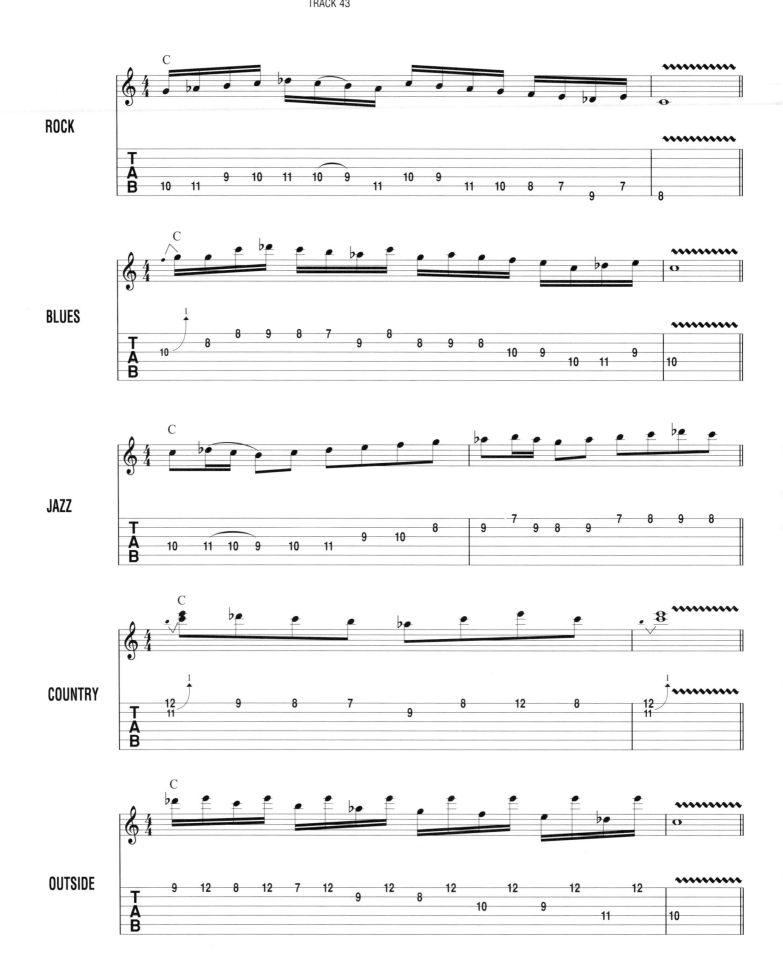

ROCK

BLUES

JAZZ

COUNTRY

OUTSIDE

LICK 44

TRACK 44

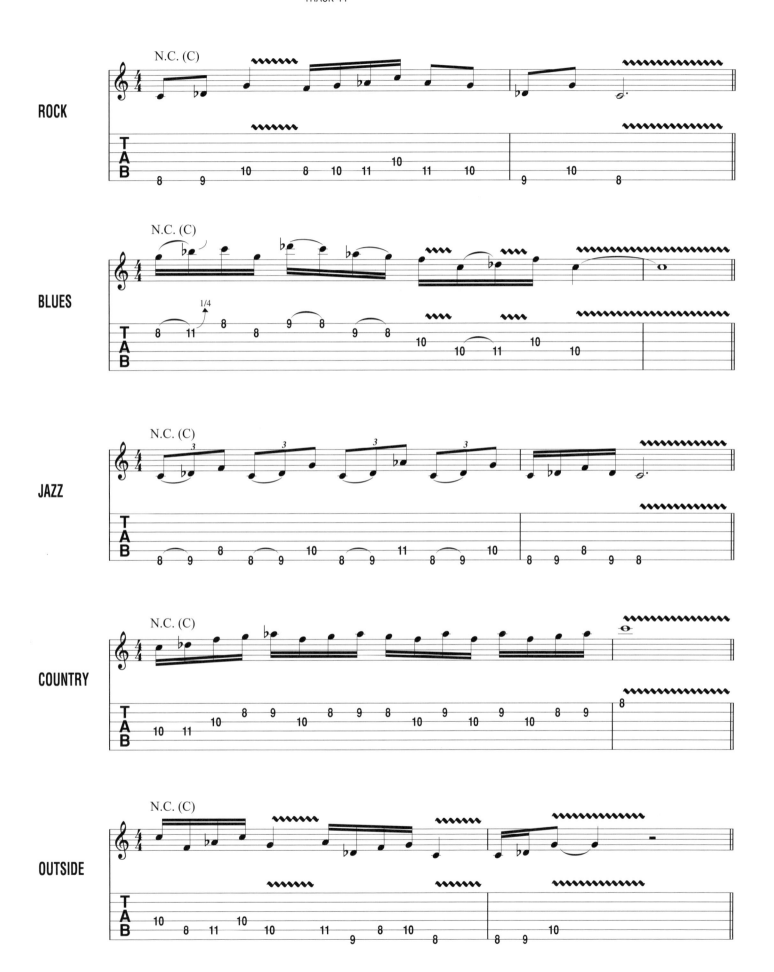

HAL LEONARD GUITAR METHOD

METHOD BOOKS, SONGBOOKS AND REFERENCE BOOKS

THE HAL LEONARD GUITAR METHOD is designed for anyone just learning to play acoustic or electric guitar. It is based on years of teaching guitar students of all ages, and it also reflects some of the best guitar teaching ideas from around the world. This comprehensive method includes: A learning sequence carefully paced with clear instructions; popular songs which increase the incentive to learn to play; versatility – can be used as self-instruction or with a teacher; audio accompaniments so that students have fun and sound great while practicing.

BOOK 1
00699010	Book Only	$8.99
00699027	Book/Online Audio	$12.99
00697341	Book/Online Audio + DVD	$24.99
00697318	DVD Only	$19.99
00155480	Deluxe Beginner Edition (Book, CD, DVD, Online Audio/ Video & Chord Poster)	$19.99

COMPLETE (BOOKS 1, 2 & 3)
00699040	Book Only	$16.99
00697342	Book/Online Audio	$24.99

BOOK 2
00699020	Book Only	$8.99
00697313	Book/Online Audio	$12.99

BOOK 3
00699030	Book Only	$8.99
00697316	Book/Online Audio	$12.99

Prices, contents and availability subject to change without notice.

STYLISTIC METHODS

ACOUSTIC GUITAR
00697347	Method Book/Online Audio	$17.99
00237969	Songbook/Online Audio	$16.99

BLUEGRASS GUITAR
00697405	Method Book/Online Audio	$16.99

BLUES GUITAR
00697326	Method Book/Online Audio (9" x 12")	$16.99
00697344	Method Book/Online Audio (6" x 9")	$15.99
00697385	Songbook/Online Audio (9" x 12")	$14.99
00248636	Kids Method Book/Online Audio	$12.99

BRAZILIAN GUITAR
00697415	Method Book/Online Audio	$17.99

CHRISTIAN GUITAR
00695947	Method Book/Online Audio	$16.99
00697408	Songbook/CD Pack	$14.99

CLASSICAL GUITAR
00697376	Method Book/Online Audio	$15.99

COUNTRY GUITAR
00697337	Method Book/Online Audio	$22.99
00697400	Songbook/Online Audio	$19.99

FINGERSTYLE GUITAR
00697378	Method Book/Online Audio	$21.99
00697432	Songbook/Online Audio	$16.99

FLAMENCO GUITAR
00697363	Method Book/Online Audio	$15.99

FOLK GUITAR
00697414	Method Book/Online Audio	$16.99

JAZZ GUITAR
00695359	Book/Online Audio	$22.99
00697386	Songbook/Online Audio	$15.99

JAZZ-ROCK FUSION
00697387	Book/Online Audio	$24.99

R&B GUITAR
00697356	Book/Online Audio	$19.99
00697433	Songbook/CD Pack	$14.99

ROCK GUITAR
00697319	Book/Online Audio	$16.99
00697383	Songbook/Online Audio	$16.99

ROCKABILLY GUITAR
00697407	Book/Online Audio	$16.99

OTHER METHOD BOOKS

BARITONE GUITAR METHOD
00242055	Book/Online Audio	$12.99

GUITAR FOR KIDS
00865003	Method Book 1/Online Audio	$12.99
00697402	Songbook/Online Audio	$9.99
00128437	Method Book 2/Online Audio	$12.99

MUSIC THEORY FOR GUITARISTS
00695790	Book/Online Audio	$19.99

TENOR GUITAR METHOD
00148330	Book/Online Audio	$12.99

12-STRING GUITAR METHOD
00249528	Book/Online Audio	$19.99

METHOD SUPPLEMENTS

ARPEGGIO FINDER
00697352	6" x 9" Edition	$6.99
00697351	9" x 12" Edition	$9.99

BARRE CHORDS
00697406	Book/Online Audio	$14.99

CHORD, SCALE & ARPEGGIO FINDER
00697410	Book Only	$19.99

GUITAR TECHNIQUES
00697389	Book/Online Audio	$16.99

INCREDIBLE CHORD FINDER
00697200	6" x 9" Edition	$7.99
00697208	9" x 12" Edition	$7.99

INCREDIBLE SCALE FINDER
00695568	6" x 9" Edition	$9.99
00695490	9" x 12" Edition	$9.99

LEAD LICKS
00697345	Book/Online Audio	$10.99

RHYTHM RIFFS
00697346	Book/Online Audio	$14.99

SONGBOOKS

CLASSICAL GUITAR PIECES
00697388	Book/Online Audio	$9.99

EASY POP MELODIES
00697281	Book Only	$7.99
00697440	Book/Online Audio	$14.99

(MORE) EASY POP MELODIES
00697280	Book Only	$6.99
00697269	Book/Online Audio	$14.99

(EVEN MORE) EASY POP MELODIES
00699154	Book Only	$6.99
00697439	Book/Online Audio	$14.99

EASY POP RHYTHMS
00697336	Book Only	$7.99
00697441	Book/Online Audio	$14.99

(MORE) EASY POP RHYTHMS
00697338	Book Only	$7.99
00697322	Book/Online Audio	$14.99

(EVEN MORE) EASY POP RHYTHMS
00697340	Book Only	$7.99
00697323	Book/Online Audio	$14.99

EASY POP CHRISTMAS MELODIES
00697417	Book Only	$9.99
00697416	Book/Online Audio	$14.99

EASY POP CHRISTMAS RHYTHMS
00278177	Book Only	$6.99
00278175	Book/Online Audio	$14.99

EASY SOLO GUITAR PIECES
00110407	Book Only	$9.99

REFERENCE

GUITAR PRACTICE PLANNER
00697401	Book Only	$5.99

GUITAR SETUP & MAINTENANCE
00697427	6" x 9" Edition	$14.99
00697421	9" x 12" Edition	$12.99

For more info, songlists, or to purchase these and more books from your favorite music retailer, go to

halleonard.com

HAL•LEONARD®